SURVIVORS

Into the Wilderness

BROWN
BEAR
BOOKS

Published in 2011 by Brown Bear Books Limited

Copyright © Brown Bear Books Limited

Brown Bear Books Limited
4877 N. Circulo Bujia
Tucson, AZ 85718
USA
and
First Floor,
9–17 St. Albans Place
London
N1 0NX

Brown Bear Books Limited
Editor: Tim Cooke
Designer: Joanne Mitchell
Picture researcher: Clare Newman
Art director: Jeni Child
Editorial director: Lindsey Lowe
Production director: Alastair Gourlay
Children's publisher: Anne O'Daly

Library of Congress Cataloging-in-Publication data available on request

ISBN: 978-0-936333-27-1

Printed in China

PICTURE ACKNOWLEDGMENTS

Front Cover: iStockphoto

Interior: Corbis: Kirk Aeder/Icon Sml 12, Oriol Alamany 29t, Frans Lemmens 14/15, Reuters 24tr, Ted Soqui 10bl; **iStockphoto:** Peter Booth 31, Sam Burt 3, Jens Carston Roseman 6/7, Adrian Dracup 5tr, Richard Gunion 10/11, Michael Svoboda 5br; **Press Association:** Associated Press 6bl, 27bl; **Rex Features:** Sipa Press 21tr; **Shutterstock:** Agrosse 28b, AP Design 28/29, Joel Bauchat Grant 26bl, Natalia Bratslowsky 24/25, EcoPrint 14c, Eric Gevaert 12/13, Simon Gurney 8/9, Chris Howey 22/23, Jessmine 10br, Jenny Leonard 20bl, Ralph Loesche 26/27, Julie Lucht 12b, Ch. Oleksandr 25tr, Dr Morley Read 20/21, Alexander Yu Zotov 4/5; **The Kobal Collection:** 20th Century Fox/Dreamworks 9t; **Thinkstock:** 16/17, 18/19; **Topham:** 5cr, 16bl, 17t, 18c, 22bl, 23tr, Caro Fotoagenture/Bastian 6tr, HIP 15cl, Pitcairn-Knowles 19b, The Granger Collection 8.

CONTENTS

SURVIVAL SKILLS

Explorers expect danger when they trek into the wilderness. But even everyday events can turn into a fight for survival. Planes crash in the mountains. Skiers and hikers lose their way. But what makes a survivor?

SURVIVAL OF THE FITTEST?

It's not about how tough or strong you are. In May 2009, three-year-old Joshua Childers wandered into a Missouri forest in a T-shirt, diaper, and trainers. He survived alone for three days and two nights in cold, pouring rain. Many adults would have died.

KEEPING A COOL HEAD

Survivors keep their wits when things go wrong. Paul Templar didn't panic when a hippo tried to swallow him. Survivors don't take stupid risks. They take time to rest, like Mauro Prosperi, who got lost in the Sahara Desert. Experience helps, though. Explorer Ernest Shackleton needed all of his to save his men from the Antarctic ice.

STAY ALIVE!

Many survivors simply refuse to die. After a giant earthquake struck China in May 2008, Ma Yuanjiang survived for seven days buried under rubble by drinking his own urine and eating paper.

△ People have survived some of the most inhospitable environments on Earth.

△ **Top**: Medics care for an injured climber. **Center**: Ernest Shackleton's ship Endurance was stuck fast in the Antarctic ice. **Bottom**: A survivor is winched to safety by a rescue helicopter.

ADRIFT ON THE OCEAN

On January 29, 1982, Steve Callahan set sail from the Canary Islands into the Atlantic. He knew the risks. Spend enough time at sea, and one day you will meet a storm. But Steve believed his yacht, *Napoleon Solo*, could survive most seas. He had built it himself!

△ *Often people try to cross stretches of open ocean on vessels that are far less seaworthy than Steve Callahan's lifeboat.*

△ *Steve named his rubber dinghy* Rubber Ducky III. *It was barely big enough for one man—but it kept him alive.*

SHIPWRECK!

Seven days out, the *Napoleon Solo* hit something. Was it a whale? Water poured in. The yacht became swamped. Steve inflated his lifeboat and jumped in. By dawn, the *Napoleon Solo* and the lifeboat had drifted apart. But Steve had had time to dive below deck to grab his emergency kit. It contained a knife, charts, tools, and a sleeping bag.

SPEAR-FISHING

For 76 days Steve floated in the ocean. Stormy seas threatened to swamp his tiny craft. The sun burned his skin. Sores soon covered his body. The food ran out, but Steve made a spear to catch fish and seabirds. He fought off sharks that attacked his dinghy. When it sprang a leak, Steve kept it afloat. He drifted almost 1,800 miles (3,000 km) before he was spotted by a fishing boat near Guadeloupe, in the Antilles islands. Steve had lost a third of his body weight … but he was alive.

SURVIVAL SKILLS

The ocean is a desert. Drinking seawater just makes you thirsty—and sick. So Steve Callahan collected rainwater in a piece of sail. He also collected water droplets from the damp air in a sail. Other sailors have survived by drinking the small amounts of liquid in fish eyes or turtles' blood.

CASTAWAY

In 1704, Scottish sailor Alexander Selkirk was first mate on the buccaneer galley *Cinque Ports* in the South Pacific. One night he argued with the captain and demanded to be put ashore. His wish was granted, and Selkirk was left stranded on the island of Juan Fernández.

ME, MYSELF, AND I

For the next four years, Alexander lived alone. All he had with him was a musket, gunpowder, carpenter's tools, a knife, a Bible, and some clothing. At first, Alexander camped in a small cave. He lived on shellfish and spent the day looking out to sea. The months passed, but no ships came.

HUNTING FOR FOOD

Later, herds of noisy sea lions drove him away from the beach. Alexander learned how to make the most of what was around him. He built two huts from trees and used his musket to hunt wild goats that lived on the island. When his gunpowder ran out, he chased the goats on foot.

△ *Selkirk did build a hut and keep goats—but it wasn't as much fun as this old picture suggests.*

△ *In the 2000 movie* Cast Away *Tom Hanks played a modern-day Selkirk. His character was stranded on an island after his plane crashed.*

RESCUED!

Alexander was finally picked up in February 1709 by another buccaneer ship, the *Duke*. The crew were starving, so Alexander hunted goats for them. When Alexander returned to England, his story provided the inspiration for Daniel Defoe's famous novel *Robinson Crusoe* (1719). But Alexander never settled back into life on land and joined the Royal Navy in 1720. A year later he fell sick and died at sea.

SURVIVAL SKILLS

Survivors have to use anything they can find. When his clothes wore out, Alexander Selkirk used a nail to sew together new clothes made from goat skins. He also made a knife out of metal barrel rings he found on the beach.

ONE LAST RIDE

On February 6, 2004, Eric LeMarque set out for a day of snowboarding in California's Sierra Nevada Mountains. The former Olympic hockey player was tough, fit—and foolish. A storm forced the local ski patrol to shut down the slopes. Eric ignored them. He wanted to have one last ride.

LOST IN THE FOG

Eric snowboarded straight into thick fog. Now lost, he had to spend the night on the mountain. The next morning, he stopped to drink at a stream. Suddenly, the bank gave way. The rushing water almost dragged him down an 80-foot (24-meter) waterfall. Eric got to the side of the river, but he was freezing cold and completely soaked. By morning, his feet were purple and black. Frostbite!

△ Eric's adventure cost him both his feet, which were badly frostbitten.

△ An MP3 player helped save Eric's life. Its radio signal showed him which way to go.

SURVIVAL SKILLS

Eric was completely unprepared for the conditions. He set off wearing light clothes and had just four pieces of gum for food. But he learned to adapt. Eric dug a snow cave with his snowboard. He also used his board to cut off tree bark. He stuffed this between his body and the snow-covered earth to keep himself warm.

AN UPHILL STRUGGLE

Eric struggled on. His feet were frozen solid. So for three days he pulled himself up the mountain with his arms. Time and again, he slipped back down. He was exhausted and starving. But Eric refused to give up. To find his way, he used the signal from his MP3 player's radio. Then he heard that a search party was looking for him. After eight days on the mountain, Eric was found. Although his badly frostbitten feet had to be cut off, Eric still loves to snowboard.

11

SHARK ATTACK

Bethany Hamilton dreamed of being a champion surfer. She had already won several events when, in 2003, the 13-year-old was surfing off Kauai island, Hawaii. While she lay on her board, a giant shadow darted under the water ... a shark!

JAWS!

Bethany felt something powerful gripping and tugging at her. A 15-foot (4.5-meter) tiger shark had bitten off her left arm, almost up to her shoulder. The water around the board turned scarlet. It had all happened so fast. Bethany was in shock. Instead of panicking, she paddled over to her friends and said, "I just got attacked by a shark."

◁ Bethany Hamilton was back on her board within a month of losing her arm to a shark attack.

SURVIVAL SKILLS

Shark attacks are actually rare. The best defense is to avoid swimming in places where they live. But if you do get attacked, fight back! Sharks look tough but they don't like to get hurt. They have been scared off by punches and kicks. When Australian diver Eric Nerhus was bitten by a shark, he gave his attacker a poke in the eye. The shark opened its mouth and Eric wriggled out.

▽ The best way to avoid sharks is not to swim in places where they are likely to be!

SHARKS
NO SWIMMING

A RACE TO THE BEACH

Although the shore was 440 yards (400 meters) away, a voice in Bethany's head told her, "Get to the beach." She was terrified the shark would return. Helped by her friends, she made it. By now the pain was making her pass out. An ambulance rushed her to the hospital, where the doctors saved her life. Most people thought she would never surf again. Bethany had other ideas. She was soon back on her board … and now she lives her dream as a pro surfer.

MANGLED BY A HIPPO

Hippos may look cute but they're deadly killers. Male hippos are especially bad-tempered. They're also armed with four giant teeth that grind against each other to keep them razor sharp. On March 9, 1996, a male hippo nearly swallowed river guide Paul Templar.

▽ *A hippo's mouth can open 4 feet (1.2 meters) wide and its teeth are always razor sharp.*

SURPRISE ATTACK

Paul led canoe trips on the Zambezi, one of Africa's longest rivers. On one trip, Paul led the canoes through a group of rocky islands. As always, he tapped his canoe to let any hippos under the water know the canoes were coming. Wham! A male hippo smacked into one of the canoes. Evans Namasango, another guide, was thrown into the water. Paul quickly paddled over to see if he could help.

▽ *This illustration from an 1883 book shows the explorer David Livingstone being attacked by a hippo on a river in Africa.*

MUNCHED!

Now the hippo lunged out of the water. It swallowed Paul up to his waist then dived back under. Paul thought to himself, "It's dark in here." He pulled himself free but the hippo wasn't done. Again and again, it chewed at Paul and pulled him under until it gave up and swam away. Paul was a mess. It took the doctor seven hours to patch up his mangled body. He lost his arm, but he was lucky. Evans Namasango's body was found in the river two days later.

SURVIVAL SKILLS

How do you fight a hippo? Paul did his best, punching the hippo in the head. Even if you avoid those big teeth, there's a risk of drowning. A hippo is able to hold its breath underwater for six minutes. And don't be fooled by that big, wobbly body. Hippos are speedy on land, too. Your best bet is to climb a tree.

HIGH SEAS, ICY WATERS

Explorer Ernest Shackleton hoped to cross the Antarctic on foot. But in January 1915, his ship was trapped in the ice. Over 10 months, it was slowly crushed. It finally sank on November 21, 1915. Shackleton and his crew were left marooned on a frozen sea.

◁ *Shackleton's ship* Endurance *was stuck in the ice until it sank.*

A CRAZY PLAN

When the ice broke up, Shackleton and his men used small boats to sail to Elephant Island. It was solid land, but there was still no hope of rescue. The men were weak and sick. Supplies were running low. But Shackleton had never lost a man, and he wasn't going to start now. His plan: sail 870 miles (1,400 kilometers) across the stormy Atlantic in a tiny boat to get help. It was suicide. But every man volunteered to go with him. Shackleton chose five.

◁ *Shackleton's crew wave goodbye to their captain and the other volunteers as they leave Elephant Island to try to get help.*

AGAINST THE ODDS

The boat sailed through storms and 65-foot (20-meter) high waves. The six men were soaked and the cold made their bones ache. Then late one day they landed on the island of South Georgia in the South Atlantic in a gale. They had to cross a mountain range, but nothing could stop Shackleton. Some 36 hours later, he reached the whaling station on the other side of the island. And just as he promised, he returned to save all 27 of his crew.

SURVIVAL SKILLS

The men left behind on Elephant Island survived by hunting penguins and eating seaweed. Their tents were ripped apart by storms, so they lived under two upturned lifeboats. Meanwhile, Shackleton and two of the men who traveled to South Georgia used frozen coils of rope as toboggans to slide down a mountainside.

TRAPPED IN A WHITE HELL

On January 12, 1923, the trawler *Sargon* left Grimsby in England. It would be four months before Captain John Patton and his crew returned. Most people thought they were dead. In fact, they were fighting to survive in one of the world's deadliest seas.

IN THE WHITE SEA

Patton headed north. He steered his ship around the top of Norway to the White Sea. For a week the fishing was poor. Then the ship landed a huge catch. By now the vessel was running short of coal for the engines. Patton turned for home. But floating ice and bad weather pushed his ship back. When the fuel ran out, the *Sargon* began to drift.

△ Northern waters were full of fish—but there was always a danger that a ship could become stuck in the ice.

IN THE GRIP OF THE ICE

The boat was pushed toward a group of giant icebergs. Soon the *Sargon* was in the grip of a vast ice sheet. The pressure of the ice threatened to crack its hull. Then the ice split with a mighty roar. For hours, giant blocks of ice leapt into the air and crashed down again. Suddenly, the ship lurched forward. It scraped past the wall of ice and into the open ocean. The ship drifted for four days. On the fifth, a German trawler found the *Sargon* and towed it back to Iceland. From there, the ship returned to Grimsby under its own steam. Captain Patton and his men had come back from the dead!

▽ *Grimsby fishermen had a highly dangerous job. At the start of his voyage north, Patton had already stopped to rescue the crew of a sinking trawler.*

SURVIVAL SKILLS

When the coal ran out, things quickly got very cold on board the *Sargon*. To keep warm, the crew set fire to anything that would burn—ropes, nets, and even their wooden bunks.

ALONE IN THE JUNGLE

It was Christmas Eve, 1971. Julianne Koepcke and her mother chatted excitedly as they boarded Flight 508 from Lima, Peru. The 17-year-old Julianne was looking forward to seeing her father, who worked in the Amazon rain forest. But an hour into the flight, a bolt of lightning hit the plane.

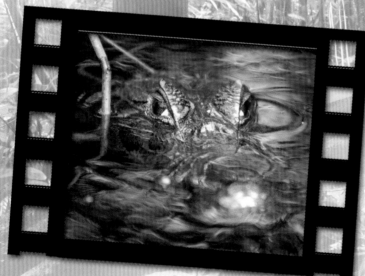

△ Although the jungle rivers were full of crocodiles, insects were a bigger danger to Julianne—they were everywhere.

FALLING FROM THE SKY

The plane broke up. Julianne went spinning to the ground. She landed still strapped into her seat, suffering a broken collarbone and cuts to her arms and legs. The teenager had no map, no tools, and no idea where she was. Sensibly, Julianne looked through the wreckage. There was no sign of her mother or any other survivors. But she did find some sweets and a Christmas cake. She took them and bravely set off into the jungle. She felt scared and very, very alone.

△ *Julianne recovered remarkably quickly from her ordeal in the jungle.*

JUNGLE PERILS

For days, Julianne waded through murky, crocodile-infested waters. Insects swarmed around her head. Blood-sucking leeches clung to her body. Maggots burrowed into the cuts on her arms. But Julianne was determined to stay alive. She built a raft out of logs and the current swept her downstream. After 10 days in the jungle, she came across a hut. The next day she was found by a team of loggers. They cleaned her wounds then took her in a canoe to the closest town. Of the 92 people on Flight 508, she was the sole survivor.

SURVIVAL SKILLS

Julianne's father had once told her that, in the jungle, rivers are like roads. If you're lost, find a small stream and follow it downhill. You will probably find a small village in a few days. But watch out for rapids and waterfalls… and crocodiles!

LOST IN THE ANDES

On October 13, 1972, a small aircraft set off from Montevideo in Uruguay. The aircraft was Uruguayan Air Force Flight 571. It was carrying 45 people. They were a rugby team and its supporters. Somewhere over the Andes Mountains, the plane crashed. The left wing and tail section were ripped off. The fuselage crash-landed on a snowy mountain slope.

BATTLE TO SURVIVE

Twelve people were killed in the crash. Others died from their injuries. Later, eight people were swept away by an avalanche. The survivors battled freezing temperatures. They had very little food and no heat. Some of the group had bad injuries from the crash and could not move. They had to stay with the plane. Then the survivors heard on the radio that the rescue search had been called off. Now they knew they were on their own.

◁ *Many of the passengers were rugby players. Perhaps being young, fit athletes helped some of them to survive their ordeal.*

△ *The survivors used the crashed body of the plane for shelter.*

SURVIVAL SKILLS

The survivors lived for nearly two months on chocolate, snacks, and candy. They melted snow to get drinking water. There were no plants or animals to eat. Food was running out. The survivors talked about what they could do. They agreed that they would have to eat flesh from the dead passengers. This sounds terrible, but what would you do in their situation?

WALK FOR HELP

In the end, 19-year-old Roberto Canessa and 21-year-old Fernando Perrado set out to get help. They hiked for 10 days across the mountains. Finally they met a man on a horse, who raised the alarm. On December 22, helicopters arrived at the scene of the crash and took six people away. The next day the last of the 16 survivors were flown to safety.

A PAINFUL ESCAPE

Aron Ralston is a born daredevil. He has fought a bear, nearly drowned, and once walked into an avalanche. On May 1, 2003, Aron went climbing in Canyonlands National Park in Utah, USA. He was scrambling along a canyon when an 800-lb (360-kilogram) boulder rolled on top of his arm.

△ Aron Ralston didn't let his accident stop him: two years later he was climbing again.

TRAPPED!

Aron was trapped. He hadn't told anyone his plans, so there was no hope of being rescued. Aron tried to chip away at the cliff with a knife. No luck. Then he tried to shift the boulder with his climbing gear. The boulder didn't budge.

By the third day, Aron's water was running out. He knew that he would die if he did not cut off his trapped arm. But his knife was too blunt.

A TERRIBLE CHOICE

Two days later, Aron tried breaking his bones before he cut through his arm. It took an hour of agony, but at last he was free. He crawled along the canyon. Using just one arm, he rigged his ropes and lowered himself down a 65-foot (20-meter) cliff. Four hours later he met some hikers, who called a rescue helicopter. Aron had survived.

In 2010, Aron's remarkable story of survival against the odds was told in the hit movie *127 Hours*, directed by Danny Boyle.

△ Aron's knife was blunt and couldn't cut through the bones and tendons in his arm.

SURVIVAL SKILLS

How did Aron make his escape? First, he worked out how to use his body weight to snap his arm bones against the rock. He used his shorts for padding. Then he used the blunt knife to cut through his flesh. Finally he used a pair of pliers to cut through his tendons. Survivor's tip: tell people where you are headed!

SCORCHED!

The Australian Outback is beautiful but it can be deadly. Without clothes, water, and shade in the morning, you could easily be dead by evening. In 2006, Ricky Megee stumbled out of the bush after being lost for 10 weeks!

LOST IN THE OUTBACK

Ricky's car broke down. The next thing he could remember was waking up, face down, in a hole. Four dingoes were scratching at the rocks, trying to get at him. He scared them off, but soon he was desperate for a drink. With no other choice, Ricky drank his own urine. It tasted foul! He was hungry, too. Ricky hunted for grubs in a tree hollow. Ouch! He got stung by a giant centipede. Soon his whole arm was swollen and painful.

◁ *The Outback is home to all sorts of frogs. Ricky found that they tasted better if they were crisped by the desert sun.*

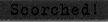

BUSH TUCKER

Ricky's luck changed when he stumbled on a natural dam. For 10 weeks, he lived on leeches, caterpillars, and grasshoppers. He cooked frogs by leaving them out in the sun until they were crispy. After 60 days, he was weak. His mouth was in agony. Using a piece of fence wire, he yanked out a rotten tooth. A few days later, when he was looking for food, Ricky stumbled into the path of a jeep. He had survived 71 days in the bush.

SURVIVAL SKILLS

Australian Aborigines are famous for their survival skills. In the past, they hunted animals (such as kangaroos, lizards, and parrots) with spears and boomerangs. They caught fish by making dams in rivers. They knew where to find bush food, or "tucker," such as berries, roots, and grubs. They ate food raw, or made fire by rubbing two sticks together.

◁ *When Ricky was found, he had lost half of his body weight, despite feeding himself on bush food.*

RUNNING INTO TROUBLE

In 1994, Italian policeman Mauro Prosperi entered the famous "Marathon of the Sands." This race across the Sahara in Africa is 140 miles (230 kilometers) long. After three days, Mauro wasn't far behind the leaders. Then a fierce sandstorm whipped across the desert. Mauro kept on running—but in the wrong direction.

HELP!

All the other runners reached the next checkpoint. But there was no sign of Mauro. For a day or so, he waited in the desert for help. On the fourth day, he spotted an airplane. Mauro spelled out "SOS" with his gear, but the plane flew away. By now, his food and water had run out. Mauro thought he was going to die. But he kept going. He was determined to see his family again.

△ The heat isn't the only danger in the Sahara—it also has poisonous snakes and deadly scorpions.

◁ *Sandstorms can whip up from nowhere and obscure everything in the desert.*

LUCKY RESCUE

Mauro survived by drinking his own urine and eating bats, snakes, and lizards. After nine days he came across a waterhole, or oasis. Soon afterward, he was found by nomads. By now Mauro was 100 miles (160 kilometers) off-course! He had wandered into Algeria, so the police thought he was a spy. They took him to a military base, then to a hospital. Mauro had survived by a miracle … and ran the race three more times!

SURVIVAL SKILLS

Temperatures can reached a scorching 122 °F (50 °C) in the Sahara. The sun burns your skin. You sweat so much that your body loses water even in the shade. But at night, temperatures can drop below 32 °F (0 °C). Mauro survived by resting in the shade of cliffs during the day. In the cold nights, he buried his body in the sand.

GLOSSARY

aborigine the original inhabitant of a country. Aboriginal peoples were living in Australia for many thousands of years before European settlers arrived in the 18th century.

avalanche a rapid fall of snow down a mountain slope, which can travel at speeds up to 185 miles per hour (300 kilometers per hour).

buccaneer another name for a pirate based in the Caribbean.

bush tucker food gathered or hunted by Aborigines and others in the Australian outback, or "bush."

cannibal someone who eats human flesh.

castaway a sailor who is cast adrift or ashore, usually as the result of a shipwreck.

daredevil a reckless person or someone who makes a living by taking risks.

dingo a wild dog found in Australia.

frostbite the damage to your body when it freezes. The skin becomes black and swollen and badly damaged areas such as fingers and toes may have to be cut off.

fuselage the main body of an aircraft that contains the cockpit, cabins, and cargo hold.

gale a very strong wind blowing at speeds over 50 miles per hour (80 kilometers per hour).

iceberg a large chunk of ice floating in the ocean, which has usually broken off from a glacier. A large iceberg can sink a ship that crashes into it.

inflate to blow up with air.

leech a wormlike creature that attaches itself to people's arms and legs and sucks their blood.

life raft a raft used in an emergency, such as when a ship is sinking.

maggots the wormlike young of flies, which are often found in rotting flesh and waste.

marathon a runing race that takes place over 26 miles 385 yards (about 40 kilometers).

marooned to be left stranded, either on purpose or by accident.

oasis a waterhole in the middle of a desert, usually created by an underground spring.

ordeal a difficult or horrible experience.

outback the dry wilderness in the middle of Australia.

sandstorm a windstorm that lifts up clouds of dust or sand.

FURTHER READING

BOOKS

Cefrey, Holly. *Steven Callahan: Adrift at Sea*. Topeka Bindery, 2003.

Chastain, Zachary. *Lost!: Surviving in the Wilderness*. Mason Crest Publishers, 2008.

Dowswell, Paul. *True Survival Stories*. Usborne Books, 2003.

Fine, Jill. *The Shackleton Expedition*. Turtleback, 2002.

Jeffrey, Gary. *Defying Death in the Desert* (Graphic Survival Stories). Evans Brothers, 2010.

Markovics, Joyce. *Blitzed by a Blizzard* (Disaster Survivors). Bearport Publishing, 2010.

Morris, Deborah. *Teens 911: Snowbound, Helicopter Crash and Other True Survival Stories*. HCI Teens, 2002.

O'Shei, Tim. *Stranded in the Snow! Eric LeMarque's Story of Survival*. Capstone Press, 2007.

Reingold, Adam. *Leveled by an Earthquake!* (Disaster Survivors). Bearport Publishing, 2010.

Roza, Greg. *Earthquake: True Stories of Survival* (Survivor Stories). Rosen Central, 2007.

Shone, Rob. *Defying Death in the Mountains* (Graphic Survival Stories). Evans Brothers Ltd., 2010.

Shone, Rob. *Defying Death in the Wilderness* (Graphic Survival Stories). Evans Brothers Ltd., 2010.

Silate, Jennifer. *Terrorist Attack: True Stories of Survival*. Rosen Publishing Group, 2007.

Spalding, Frank. *Plane Crash: True Stories of Survival*. Rosen Central, 2007.

Sunna, Ellyn. *Nature's Wrath: Surviving Natural Disasters*. Mason Crest Publishers, 2000.

WEBSITES

http://adventure.howstuffworks.com/survival/wilderness/survival.htm
The How Stuff Works guide to 10 Harrowing Survival Stories.

http://www.equipped.com/srvstoriestoc.htm
A collection of true life survival stories.

http://www.guardian.co.uk/culture/gallery/2010/oct/17/ten-best-survival-stories
Web site of the Guardian newspaper with its choice of courageous tales of survival.

http://wildernesssurvivalstories.com
A collection of unedited personal accounts from throughout the United States.

http://www.rd.com/survival-stories
Reader's Digest pages featuring miraculous true survival stories.

http://www.nationalgeographic.com/adventure/alive/survivors-expedition.html
National Geographic Adventure magazine's site about the survivors of the Andes plane crash.

INDEX

Numbers in *italics* refer to illustrations.